Dog Park Basics

CASSIE LEIGH

Copyright © 2015 M.L. Humphrey

All rights reserved.

ISBN: 978-1-950902-59-0

Also published under ISBN 978-1533504203 and previously published as Dog Park Primer ISBN: 1517209897

TITLES BY CASSIE LEIGH

DOG-RELATED
Puppy Parenting Basics
Puppy Parenting in an Apartment
Dog Park Basics

COOKING-RELATED
You Can't Eat the Pretty

DATING FOR WOMEN
Online Dating for Women: The Basics
Online Dating is Hell

DATING FOR MEN
Online Dating for Men: The Basics
Don't Be a Douchebag
You Have a Date, Don't F It Up
The How to Meet a Woman Collection

CONTENTS

Introduction	1
Not All Dog Parks Are The Same	5
How Do You Find Dog Parks?	13
Things To Think About When Choosing A Dog Park	15
Preparing For The Park	19
Dog Park Etiquette	21
When To Take Your Dog	29
Dog Parks Aren't Just For Perfectly Healthy Dogs	31
Understanding Potential Hazards	33
Not All Dog Owners Are Nice People	37
Friendly Owner, Friendly Dog	41
Signs Of A Dangerous Or Upset Dog	43
Dogs Playing With Other Dogs At The Dog Park	47
The Jumping Dog	51
Disciplining Other People's Dogs	53
Post-Park Care	55
Conclusion	59

INTRODUCTION

Growing up we always had dogs, but it never even occurred to us to take them to a dog park. Honestly, I'm not even sure dog parks existed back then. They certainly didn't exist in the town of a hundred people I started out in. Maybe they existed somewhere when I was older and living in a larger metropolitan area, but, if they did, I didn't know about it.

And we certainly didn't take our dogs there.

Our dogs were house dogs for the most part. We usually had two or three the whole time I was growing up and they spent their days in the house and in the yard. That's just the way it was and I never questioned it.

I might occasionally take one for a walk in the nearby park, but that was taking her on-leash with me when I went for a walk. It wasn't about finding a place for her to play and let off some steam.

Fast-forward twenty years and I'm well into adulthood and haven't had a dog that whole time and I end up with a puppy I hadn't planned on owning. (Long story, short: My mom bought a puppy for herself. Her older dog attacked the puppy two days later. Mom offered me the pup or said she'd have to take it back. I took the puppy and ended up changing my life completely as a result.)

So, there I was. New puppy with lots of energy and living in an apartment. Now, at first, I just walked the pup around the apartment complex and took her to a neighboring sports facility with four big soccer fields side-by-side where, during the day, she could run around off-leash. I also took her to PetSmart once or twice a week for a few hours so she could play with other puppies.

(Once she was old enough for that to be safe. It's not safe for a new puppy to be near a lot of other dogs until it has most of its shots. That includes day care and the dog park.)

I quickly realized that pup loved the outdoors and needed a chance to really run around somewhere. Walking on leash with me just wasn't enough no matter how long the walk. (And pup liked EPIC walks sometimes. Like that one time in the middle of a snowstorm that shut down the entire city when we were outside for a good hour and a half…Good times.)

It really hit home for me when we moved to the Washington, DC area and were living in Crystal City where it's mostly busy streets and lots of traffic. (My old apartment was full of large grassy courtyards. My DC apartment? Not so much. There was a four foot by twenty foot area around the side of the building where I could take the pup to do her business, but otherwise we had to walk about eight blocks to get to a park-like area. Even then, it was not somewhere I could just let her run loose. Although people did and I sometimes did. It was always a heart attack moment, though, worrying she'd go the other direction and run across four lanes of traffic.)

(Something she did at least twice after slipping out of her collar…)

So, anyway. There we were in DC. I had a six-month-old, energetic puppy who wanted to walk for an hour or so each time we left the building. And who wasn't getting as much puppy play time as she should've been. (Although we did occasionally have a little play session in the lobby with one of her puppy friends. Something that amused the front desk staff, fortunately, but didn't really please the other residents in the building.)

Enter the dog park.

There were tons of them in the DC area. Well, okay, maybe not tons. But a good ten or fifteen that were within a half hour's drive.

Pup and I set out to explore most of them. We developed our favorites, like Glencarlyn, and we also developed our never-go-there-agains. (There were many, unfortunately. Mostly because of the bad vibe I'd get when I took the pup there. No matter how cute your puppy is, when she's sixty-five pounds plus there will always be a few haters out there. And some people are just very territorial about their park like it was built especially for them.)

When we returned to Colorado we actually moved into a house with a yard, but...

It wasn't enough for the pup. Oh, sure, she'll take what you give her. If I'd decided she was never leaving the confines of the yard ever again, she would've probably accepted it with her quiet little pout and sad eyes and still given me puppy kisses and occasionally let me get close enough to snuggle with. But she would've been sad and missed getting to run around and swim and play with other dogs.

So, we set out to see what was around here. Seems to me there are fewer options in Colorado than there were in DC, which is interesting because I think Colorado is more dog-friendly in general than DC was. (At least in our experience.)

But we've tried out a handful of places and found two favorites. One nearby that we can go to daily and one about forty minutes away that I really like but can't be a daily trip for us.

Along the way I've developed some impressions and opinions about dog parks, the types of people that go there, and the things you should keep in mind when taking your dog to one. That's what the rest of this book is about. It's a general guide to taking your dog to the dog park.

Do you NEED it? No. You can do what I did and just show up at each dog park and wing it. Will it help, though? I certainly hope so or I wouldn't have bothered to write it.

It's a practical guide, by the way. Maybe someday I'll write a book of all my weird encounters at various dog parks (some of those did sneak their way in), but for now I just want to share what I've learned.

So, let's talk dog parks, shall we?

NOT ALL DOG PARKS ARE THE SAME

The first thing you have to realize is that not all dog parks are the same. They can range from small barren areas surrounded by a chain-metal fence to hundreds of acres of untamed wilderness that's only partially fenced. And whether a particular park actually works for you and your dog will very much depend on you, your dog, and what you're hoping to get out of the experience.

It's also very dependent on the other people and dogs that are there when you go. Which means you can have a great experience at a park one time and a horrible experience the next time.

This just happened to me and the pup at the park we go to almost daily. There were a lot of dogs that aren't normally there because it was a weekend and, I don't know, maybe something was in the air, but we ran into two dog fights. Not serious ones, but serious enough to not be enjoyable. (Pup has a bad habit of running towards a dog fight instead of away from it...Like she can somehow get everyone to just get along if she tries hard enough.)

The first thing you should do when you go to any new dog park, is keep your eyes open to see what the place is like. Is it clean? What type of dogs are there? How do the owners behave?

I've been to some parks that I knew I'd never go back to after one visit. There was one that was basically sand surrounded by a fence. The dogs and owners were fine, but the pup came away covered in a fine layer of grit and there was really nothing there for her to do. It just wasn't nice.

I've been to others where I wasn't so sure the first time. Or even where I loved it the first time and hated it the second. Sometimes you have to go to a park a few times to really decide if it works for you.

And what works for one dog probably won't work for another.

I have a large dog who likes open spaces and doing her own thing ninety percent of the time. That's why both of our favorite parks are huge open spaces where she has plenty of room to roam on her own if she wants. And I'd say the majority of the dogs I see there regularly are big dogs. Fifty-pounds plus.

My good friend owns three Chihuahuas. The one time she joined us at my normal park, I don't think she really liked it. And I don't blame her. While my dog is great with smaller dogs I have to imagine that for a small-dog owner every time a big dog approaches they have to wonder if the dog is going to attack their little one or play with them.

(Some breeds have very strong prey instincts and a small dog that moves in the wrong way can trigger that reaction in them and they'll attack. Not pleasant to think about, but you have to consider something like that if you're going to take your dog to dog parks on a regular basis. Especially if it's a small dog.)

The main differences I've noticed between dog parks fall into three general areas: the amenities they offer, the dog owners, and the dogs themselves. (Those last two often go hand in hand. Usually, friendly dog, friendly owner.)

Let's talk through some examples of different parks I've visited and why they did or didn't work for me and my pup. (Keeping in mind that each owner and dog's experience will be different):

Example 1:

The closest dog park to where I lived in DC was a hundred foot by forty foot area next to a tennis court. It theoretically had a small-dog area (that looked like it wasn't even usable), an agility course, and some trees. I want to say that it didn't have any water available on-site, but that could be because it was winter.

(You'll find that most dog parks don't provide water during the winter months if you're in an area where water pipes can freeze.)

Now, my dog was about sixty pounds at the time, so I didn't really need a small dog area for her. If she had been small, I doubt that small dog area would've worked for me because it was a six foot by six foot space and in bad repair.

The agility course, which was a wooden ramp or two, didn't do anything for me or the pup. Beyond training my dog in how to obey basic commands, I've never felt a need to train her to do anything else. (She doesn't even shake hands which seems to shock and appall strangers.)

So, it was just a shady, decent-sized area that was mostly dirt with traces of grass and that I could reach in fifteen minutes or so. It was also never really busy, which was nice, but sometimes there were no other dogs there at all, which wasn't. At six-months-old my dog was still looking for other dogs to play with.

The people were, almost always, really nice. (I had one *weird* experience there that caused me to never go back, but that was an exception, not the norm for that place.)

Verdict? It was fine in a pinch, but not on the top of my list.

Now, keep in mind, as your dog matures, you may find, as I did, that your dog's needs change. After pup hit eighteen months or so she became much more selective about which dogs she'd play with. Often now a dog will try to play with her and she'll ignore it. When she was younger she wanted to play with every dog, even the ones that were snarling at her to go away.

So, when she was little I always wanted there to be other dogs around. Now, if we go to the park and don't run into anyone, that's fine, because there's enough for her to explore on her own and she doesn't really crave that sort of interaction as much.

So, that was one option I had.

Example 2:

Another was a very long but narrow dog park that people raved about. It was about twenty minutes away from us and had lots of trees and, theoretically, a stream for pup to swim in. (I think the stream was technically outside the park and down a steep hill. I'd heard that dogs cut their paws open on some of the debris on the bottom of the stream bed so we never did try it out. We only went twice.)

This park also had a puppy/small dog area, which we didn't need, but I think was a nicer space than the other park offered.

The park was mostly dirt, which meant mud if it had rained recently.

My big problem with the park was that it was *insanely* popular. I wouldn't be surprised to know that there were hundreds of dogs there the days I was there. Not only did this make parking nearby very challenging, but it also didn't work for my pup.

For a very social owner and a very social dog, it was probably great. But my pup gets scared when other dogs bark at her—even when they're trying to be friendly. She also gets a little nervous when a pack of dogs approach her. Dogs didn't tend to pack at this park the way I've seen at others, but it was just a little overwhelming.

And the owners weren't right on top of their dogs. An owner might be fifty feet away or even a hundred feet away talking to someone else. There was even one guy reading a book. (You'll find that some dog owners are like that. They go to the dog park to socialize as much as they go to take their dog for exercise and some don't realize that it's important to keep an eye on your dog.)

Verdict? Not our kind of place. Far too crowded. People were nice, dogs were nice, but just too much for both of us.

Example 3:

Another place we went to was a hundred foot by hundred foot dirt area near a park.

Supposedly the local residents were really tight-knit and took good care of it and there was a great group of dogs and owners that were there regularly. (This according to a woman I met at another park. You'll find that the best way to learn about new dog parks is to talk to other dog owners when you're at the dog park.)

Our one and only experience of that dog park lasted about five minutes. We showed up, there were about five people and five or six dogs there. The people were all gathered in a circle talking. The dogs were running as a pack and ALL of them came at my dog immediately when we stepped through the gate.

She hid between my legs and cried. Now, the dogs weren't snarling or anything, but five eighty-pound dogs running at you isn't the most enjoyable experience.

Only one of the owners even bothered trying to call his dog away. The others just kept talking. Finally, one of the others noticed and did call his dog away and the other dogs followed it. But the minute pup moved away from me the dogs chased her down until she ran back between my legs.

We left.

Example 4:

The miserable experience at that last park is how we finally ended up at Glencarlyn, the park we went to most of the time we were in DC. People had been telling me about it for weeks, but I'd been really nervous about taking her there because it wasn't fenced in at all and I worried that she'd just run away from me and never come back.

I'd envisioned some park that was right off a busy road with a hill she could run up and get hit. But it wasn't like that at all. It was tucked away in the midst of a large park in a residential area. The worst I ever saw happen was a dog that liked to run up to the patios of some neighboring condos and dogs that would run into the small parking area.

Why I liked it:

The people and dogs were for the most part friendly and non-cliquish, meaning we usually were able to interact with dogs one-on-one or two at a time. I never saw dogs or owners that packed together when I was there.

There were lots of big dogs there. (I'd say almost exclusively bigger dogs, which was nice because no one gave pup the side-eye for her size.)

It had a stream the pup could play in, which for a Newfie is invaluable. She will play in a muddy puddle she loves so water so much. (She once got all excited about a flooded irrigation ditch.)

The main area was dirt, which could get muddy and did often require a quick rinse in the bath tub when we got home, but the rest of the park was forested hillside. Pup was able to run through there and leap over logs and chase squirrels and just have a ball.

Now, it wasn't perfect. Like I said, it wasn't fenced. There was the stream on one side and the hill on the other. Usually that wasn't a problem, but occasionally it did become one.

Every once in a while weird people would do things like stand on the other side of the stream and throw rocks in the water towards the dogs or stop their bikes right where the dogs were playing to rinse out their helmet. When this happened, pup would start barking or, worse yet, swim across the stream to bark at them.

Also, one day this guy walked through the middle of the dog park glaring at all the dogs and said, "I don't like dogs." (And yet, you're walking through the middle of a dog park...Hm. Okay.) Problem is, it wasn't well-labeled and sectioned-off as a dog park, so those kinds of mistakes did occur on occasion.

But, overall, it was our clear favorite. Good people, good dogs, a stream, and a forested hillside. And, of course, plenty of tennis balls.

Example 5:

Those were some of our DC experiences.

We came back here and had to go through our search all over again.

There was a park near me that I thought might be perfect. It was a big grassy area, which was fantastic because it's incredibly rare for a dog park to have nice green grass. (Dogs are just too rough on grass for it to last. This place kept it grassy by switching out sides, so only half of the park was ever open at one time.)

I also liked the area and it was close enough to be convenient. BUT.

Pup *hated* that place.

Every time we went there, dogs rushed her as soon as we arrived. And no one even tried to call them back. And the people generally weren't welcoming either. They weren't cliquish like I've seen elsewhere, they just didn't talk to anyone. They all kind of stood apart and didn't really control their dogs either.

That park had more poop per square foot than I've probably seen at any other park. It was gross, which is too bad because it was a very beautiful place if you just drove by.

So, because of the people who didn't pick up, the unfriendly owners, and the fact that pup didn't like any of the dogs there, that one was quickly scratched from our list. I'll actually walk pup around a lake on leash before I'll consider taking her there again.

Example 6:

We eventually found a couple other parks that really work for us. They have streams or lakes for the pup to play in and enough area for her to run around and get good and tired. They aren't muddy patches of land either. Both are fenced-in wilderness so mostly full of wild grasses and scrub brush.

And the people are generally friendly at both. Like I said before, pup is really more of a solo walker these days than a play-with-everyone type of dog, but at both she can occasionally run into dogs that she does want to play with.

One thing that is important to consider with both of them, though, is that there are other hazards at these parks. Pup has found snakes, frogs, badgers, and dead rodents (that she ate) at the one. I'm pretty sure I lost her to an elk chase for ten minutes at the other.

Also, in the summer months, she gets into the wild grass at the one and I have to spend about twenty minutes picking the little pokey bits out of her toes and coat when we get home.

There are also some dogs she's scared of at the one park. Not many, but a couple. And at least one person that is so obnoxious and rude that if I see him coming I try to go the other way. Fortunately, both parks are large enough that you can avoid a dog or person you want to avoid.

🐾 🐾 🐾

So, those are a few of my experiences. Why did I just subject you to that long-winded description of parks you'll probably never go to?

To help you understand that there's an incredibly wide variety of choices out there and that the closest park to you may not be the best park for you. If you really do think you want to take your dog to a dog park, explore your options. You may luck out and find the perfect park right away, but don't get discouraged if you don't.

And keep in mind that as your pup changes and maybe even you change, the right park for you will change, too.

HOW DO YOU FIND DOG PARKS?

So how do you find dog parks to even try out?

You might luck out and just see one as you're driving by. (That's how I found the one the pup hates.)

The best option is word-of-mouth. Ask your fellow dog owners where they take their dogs, especially if it's someone with a dog that has a similar temperament and size. I found a large number of the dog parks I tried in the DC area by talking to dog owners at dog parks. At least four or five people told me about Glencarlyn before I finally checked it out myself.

Ask your dog trainer or vet for recommendations. (Although I think my vet would likely recommend that I not take my pup to the park I take her to because of all the potential hazards and bacteria in the water.)

Another option is just a basic internet search for something like "dog parks arlington virginia." I tried looking at the city or the county websites for where I was, but that sometimes requires enough knowledge of your area to know whether you should look at the city or county website. (Or state in the case of one of the parks I like.) For example, I was in Alexandria, but Arlington parks were actually closer to where I was.

I also used bringfido.com when I was traveling cross-country. They list dog parks in different cities and have some user reviews as well. It led the pup and I to a couple nice parks when we were driving back from DC to Colorado.

THINGS TO THINK ABOUT WHEN CHOOSING A DOG PARK:

There are lots of variables to consider when choosing a dog park. Some information you can figure out before you even go there. If you find a website with pictures of the park you can decide if it's even worth the effort of visiting. Others you're really only going to know once you've visited a few times.

I'd encourage you to read any reviews you can find before you go, too. Reviews aren't always accurate, but a place that has nothing but five-star reviews is likely in better repair than one with mixed or no reviews.

In general, there won't be many reviews available. The park I love to take the pup to probably has twenty-five to fifty people there at any given time but only has a total of three reviews on bringfido.com. But they're all five-star, so you can tell there's something good about the place.

(You can also learn important tricks about the park. When pup and I were on the road there was one dog park that wasn't at the address given on the website. The only way I managed to find it was based upon a review that explained where to actually go to reach the park. It was a very nice place once I stopped driving around the trailer park where it wasn't.)

So, what should you think about when you're considering different dog park options?

1. Is water provided or do you need to bring your own?

2. Are poop bags provided or do you need to bring your own?

3. Is it fenced? Completely/partially?

4. Is there shade?

5. Is there grass?

6. Is it exclusively a dog park or can other activities occur there? (Like fishing, jogging, or bike riding, for example.)

7. What kind of dogs go there? Is it a big-dog park or a small-dog park?

8. What kind of people go there? Are they friendly or do they sneer at you and your dog? (Literally happened to me at one park.)

9. Do people clean up after their dogs for the most part? (You'll never see it happen 100% of the time, but most people should be taking care of things most of the time or it just gets gross fast.)

10. Do people discipline their dogs well? Do they tend to stay with their dogs or let their dogs wander out of sight?

11. How does your dog like the place?

12. How do you like it?

13. What activities are there for your dog?

14. Is there enough room for your dog to run around and have fun?

15. If you have a small dog or puppy, is there an area where your dog can play that's smaller and more protected?

16. If your dog likes to play, are there good dogs to play with?

17. If your dog prefers to just be with you, is that possible?

18. Are there any other hazards you should be aware of?

19. How much post-visit time will you need to put in to either bathe your dog or remove burrs/stickers/etc. from your dog's coat?

20. Does it cost anything to access the park? (Most don't, but the one I like requires a pass or daily fee.)

21. Do you need to have any sort of registration/shots to take your dog to the park? (Many jurisdictions require that you register your dog. Failure to do so can result in a fine.)

🐾 🐾 🐾

I know. It seems like a long list. But all of these questions address an important aspect of your overall enjoyment of the dog park.

PREPARING FOR THE PARK

Before you ever even leave the house, think about what you might need with you. I covered this a bit in the puppy parenting book, but I'll act as if you didn't read that and we're starting from scratch.

I have a "go bag" I generally carry with me when I take the pup anywhere. It includes some essentials that I almost always end up needing. For example, poop bags (because you never know when your dog is going to decide to do their business) and treats (because my dog sometimes needs to be bribed to do what I want, like leave).

I also put my phone, wallet, and keys in the bag while we're at the park. I think some people tend to leave their phone and/or wallet in their vehicle, but I would never recommend this. It's way too easy for someone to break into a car when your attention is focused on your dog, so just bring that stuff with you.

(Of course, I am a woman, so this is easier for me than it is for men, but still.)

I also carry my park pass with me for the place where I go now.

And tissues. Pup slobbers sometimes to the point of ridiculousness, and I occasionally end up pulling something out of her mouth that I'd rather not think about and rather not have on my hands for any length of time.

Many people bring one of those little plastic ball-throwers with them. Or they bring tennis balls or floaty toys that they can throw out in the water.

(I don't. Pup likes to lose balls. She either gives them to other dogs or drops them in the middle of some body of water where I can't reach them. So I rarely if ever bring toys into the dog park with me. If there's a ball there (and there almost always are at our regular park), then we'll play with it. Otherwise, we do without.)

Also, think about bringing water, especially in hot weather.

The park I take the pup to has two lakes and, during the summer months, two fountains. I don't worry about having water with me when we go there. But I've been to other parks where there was no water and it was a warm enough day that the dogs really needed something. Many parks like this are neighborhood parks and people bring jugs or buckets of water for communal use. (In that case, try to contribute if you're a regular.)

One last thing to think about is how dirty you want your car to be. Many people at the park I go to have towels in their cars to wipe their dogs down when they leave the park. Me? I just let it go. My pup jumps into the car soaking wet with her paws covered in sand or mud. It's just a losing battle I choose not to fight. But if it's one you want to fight, bring a towel.

Also, think about what the weather is like and dress accordingly. You're going to be outside for half an hour or an hour. If it's cold, wear good warm shoes and enough layers to be comfortable. If it's hot think about a hat of some sort and sunscreen. Especially if you go to a larger park where it's easy to get far away from your car.

DOG PARK ETIQUETTE

I think there are certain actions and behaviors that everyone should follow when they're at the dog park. It's a communal space meaning that the experience you have at the park is going to be significantly impacted by how others act and behave at the park.

Keep in mind, this is my personal opinion of how people should behave at the dog park and how they should control their dogs. I'm sure there are people out there that would disagree with me. (I've certainly seen people not do all the things I'm about to discuss.) But this is what I think constitutes polite behavior in a shared space when accompanied by animals that can at times be dangerous.

1. Never take a dangerous dog to the dog park

You'd think this is an obvious one. So obvious, in fact, that I left it out of the puppy parenting book. But I was at the park the other day and this woman explained to me that she was nervous when her dogs approached mine because sometimes they just went off on other dogs and she was never sure what would set them off.

These were two large dogs and I doubt she could've controlled both at once and yet there she was taking them to the dog park.

If you know that you have a dog that will attack other dogs, don't take it to the dog park. That simple.

(And, even if your dog isn't dangerous, know that there is always the chance that someone will bring a dangerous dog to the park and be alert to it. The best way to handle a situation like that is to get your dog away from the other dog before they even meet.)

2. Keep your dog leashed outside the dog park

Many people let their dogs run from their vehicles to the dog park gate without having them leashed up.

DO NOT DO THIS.

Sure, it may go well 95% of the time. But that other 5%? Your dog runs in front of a car or bicycle and gets hit or causes a scene. OR it runs up to some other dog whose owner is trying to control it and creates a problem. Just don't take that kind of risk. Especially if the parking and the dog park entrance are separated by an area where cars drive through.

Have you ever really thought about it when you're backing up your car near a dog park? It would be HARD to see some types of dogs. And if you don't have a six-foot human next to that dog, you're very likely to back right over it.

You don't want that to happen to your dog and the person who hits the dog certainly doesn't want to be responsible for something like that happening. So, keep your dog leashed from the car to the dog park entrance.

3. Drive slowly around the dog park

This is one I didn't include before because it should be obvious, but I don't think it always is: Drive slowly when you're near the dog park. First, dogs get away from their owners and you don't want to run one over. Second, it can be complete chaos at a busy dog park on a weekend with people arriving and people leaving and dogs playing and…Go slow. Especially be careful when backing up. Check your environment before you pull in or out of a parking space. If you see a person, be sure you see their dog, too, before you move.

4. Think long and hard before bringing children

I once saw a young girl knocked over by a group of playing dogs. And it was the parents' fault it happened. Not only did they bring their child, and five of her friends, to the dog park, but they let her run around in the dogs' play area. (This was a smaller park with a gravel area for the dogs and a concrete area for the owners.)

Even adults can get broadsided by playing dogs. I bet if you asked around you'd find that almost every single person who regularly goes to a dog park has at one point in time been knocked into by two playing dogs. It's happened to me more than once and I barely managed to stay standing and avoid painful knee injury. Think what that could mean for a small child.

Also, if you do bring children, you need to be in charge of how they act towards other dogs. Most dogs are fine, but if a child acts aggressively towards a dog the dog may react. I don't have kids and the pup isn't around kids a lot, which means she's not used to being treated the way some kids treat dogs. The loud screaming, the running at or away from the dog, the tugging on a tail or an ear. Any of that can lead a dog to snap at a kid.

And while I know my dog wouldn't bite a child, that is not necessarily the case with all other dogs.

Also, if you do bring a kid to the dog park, don't bring the kid's scooter or bike. When the pup was very little I had some girl in my complex ride right up into her face on a scooter. Scared the pup so bad she peed herself. Now when she sees someone on a scooter, she gets freaked out. Pup also almost got run over by a bike at the dog park once. She saw a dog she wanted to say hi to and ran right in front of the bike to get to the dog. She didn't know any better. She was in her space.

5. Control your dog

I think it's ultimately the responsibility of each dog owner to make sure that their dog behaves appropriately towards other dogs and towards any animals in the dog park.

Where I take the pup is a wild environment and there are a number of animals there like badgers and frogs and ducks. I've seen other dogs attack these animals and I just don't think that's right. I've also seen dogs attack other dogs and either the owner was nowhere nearby to stop their dog or they were incapable of taking control of their dog and ending the situation.

The best way to control your dog is to lead them away from a situation you know will be problematic before it escalates. If not, get your dog under control and leave.

And, look, it will happen at some point that your dog either initiates or reacts to another dog in a negative way. Be prepared to act when it happens.

My dog is close to a hundred pounds, but you better believe if she's on top of some other dog I'll be right there grabbing her by the back of her neck and dragging her away. That's my responsibility as her owner. If you can't handle your dog in a difficult situation, you shouldn't bring it to the dog park.

6. Be friendly to other dogs and their owners

I've found that one of the easiest ways to put a dog at ease is to greet it with a friendly tone. When dogs approach each other they don't know what they're getting. You can see it in their body language. They lower their head and wag their tail a bit and try to give off a friendly vibe without looking too weak. I've found that if the humans are relaxed and friendly the dogs will take their cue from that behavior and are more likely to be relaxed and friendly with one another.

It also makes the whole experience more pleasant if you're friendly to the dogs and owners. You don't have to get into a lengthy conversation with everyone, but just a smile and a hello go a long way.

I've definitely seen people at the dog park who approached my dog, and therefore me, with annoyance and distrust. It doesn't help things and, with my pup at least, it's misguided. She plays well with dogs of all sizes and is friendly or indifferent 99% percent of the time, so approaching her with that kind of negativity isn't helpful.

7. Ask before giving treats to other dogs

I always have a handful of treats with me to lure the pup away from the park or let me put her leash on her. Ideally, you wouldn't bring treats to a dog park because some dogs will follow you around the whole time trying to get them from you, but it's pretty common for people to have them.

If you find yourself in a situation where someone else's dog is begging for a treat from you and you want to give it one, ask permission first. Some dogs have allergies or sensitive stomachs and you giving that dog a treat can mean a very bad rest of the day for its owner. So always ask first.

(Also, some people just don't want their dogs to eat strange treats and some dogs will practically bite your hand off for a treat. Best to not do it.)

8. Do not let your dog jump on people

There always seems to be one dog at each dog park that is a very nice, lovable dog that jumps on everyone. Usually this dog is over fifty-pounds, so it can pack a wallop when it does jump on someone. And the owner is always so nice and apologetic about it. And yet, week after week, month after month, that dog continues to jump on people.

IT IS NOT OKAY to have a dog that jumps on people. Train your dog better. A few weeks of it happening as you get the dog trained, fine. The occasional slip-up when the dog just gets too danged excited. Fine. But months? No. If you can't control your dog, don't take it to the dog park.

9. If your dog takes another dog's toy, give it back

Pup generally plays with balls we find at the park, so I don't have any special attachment to any ball she's playing with. But I've known dogs that would only play with one particular ball. And they'd know the difference, too, between their special ball and another one that looked identical. So, when pup takes another dog's ball, which does happen on occasion because dogs often drop balls in front of other dogs when they meet, I try to give the ball back. Some people don't care, some do; it's always nice to make the gesture.

10. Don't get uptight about dogs being dogs

As a follow-up on the last point…Dogs will take each other's toys. Dogs will run up to one another and sniff one another. Don't take your dog to a dog park and then act like a jerk when another dog comes up to your dog or tries to join in your game of catch.

Yes, I generally try to keep pup away from those sorts of people when I see them. (They tend to be pretty obvious.) But it's a dog park. If you want one-on-one time with your dog, take them somewhere private not to a dog park where most of the dogs expect to socialize with one another and play together.

11. Pick up after your dog

This should be obvious, but given the number of times I've seen dog crap on the ground, it seems it isn't. A dog park is a shared space and it's only going to be as nice as you and other people who use it keep it. So pick up after your dog.

My basic rule is if I can reach it, I pick it up. That includes if my dog goes off the path, which she normally does.

Every once in a while pup wanders off into waist-high grass and squats down a good ten feet from the path and I don't pick up after her. I know that I could probably make it there but I'd be navigating my way through a minefield of other dogs' crap that wasn't picked up and I let it go. But dog crap right there on the path? Come on…

12. Don't litter

Previously, I had this specific to smokers and leaving cigarette butts around. But at my current park I've seen water bottles and fishing lures and who knows what else. Don't litter. Take out what you bring with you.

That includes cigarettes. Too many dogs are attracted to cigarette butts and will try to eat them. It's just not right. (And, honestly, most dog park people are not smokers. I can only think of two people I've ever seen smoking while at the dog park. So maybe just don't even do it while you're there.)

WHEN TO TAKE YOUR DOG

Give some thought about what time of day you take your dog to the park, and, even, which day of the week.

You should know your dog and what weather is comfortable for it.

For example, in the summer I only take the pup to the dog park first thing in the morning or late in the evening. Mid-day in Colorado in June is simply too hot for a dog with her kind of coat. She spends those hot mid-day hours inside in front of the air conditioning. In the winter, I can pretty much take her at any time of day, but not in the summer.

Even if your dog doesn't have a thick black coat like mine, taking a dog out in the middle of the day in hot weather is not a good idea. Dogs do get sunburned. Also, if they're walking on hot asphalt, they can blister their paws.

In the winter, if it gets too cold, dogs' feet will freeze up. And some breeds have no business being outside in the middle of winter without significant layers on. (Like my friend's Chihuahuas.)

So, know what hazards exist for *your* dog. If it's a dog with minimal or no coat, you may not want your dog out in midday because of risk of sun burn. (You can use sunscreen on them.) If your dog doesn't have much of a coat and it's winter, you may want to wait until the hottest part of the day to take it to the park.

Also, the weekend dog park crowd and the weekday crowd are very, very different.

You are much more likely to run into problematic dogs on a weekend than you are mid-week. That's because most of the people at a dog park mid-week are the regulars who have well-trained dogs and come to the park daily. People who come on the weekend are often people who only take their dog out on a weekend or people who've never been to a dog park before and are just trying it out.

Nothing wrong with that, but if you have the choice, I would recommend going to any new dog park during the week if you possibly can. And, better yet, at a time of day when most people won't be there. So, standard work hours if you can pull it off. That'll just let you and your dog get to know the park itself before you have to start dealing with all the people and dogs, too.

DOG PARKS AREN'T JUST FOR PERFECTLY HEALTHY DOGS

One more thing that I think is important to mention is that dog parks aren't just for perfectly healthy dogs. Sure, you don't want to bring a dog that can get other dogs sick. And you definitely don't want to bring an aggressive dog that will harm other dogs. But don't assume that just because your dog is old or ill that you can't take it to the dog park.

At the park I go to regularly there are at least four dogs that I see on a somewhat regular basis that are missing a limb. Those dogs don't play with the other dogs as much, but some of them do. My pup has played with at least one of them. And they do still enjoy walking around the lake with their owners.

Same goes for dogs with long-term illnesses. There's one elderly dog at my dog park that has some sort of skin condition and walks slow as can be, but that dog is at the park a few times a week with his owner. She lets him set his pace and they generally only do a short walk, but he loves it there.

I know another man whose dog had a large tumor for a number of years before it passed. He said he routinely brought that dog to the dog park.

So if your dog is capable of walking around and getting the exercise and can safely leave the house, consider taking it to a dog park. (And, obviously, make sure the park is a good fit for the dog and its activity levels and interest in other dogs and humans.)

UNDERSTANDING POTENTIAL HAZARDS

There are always risks to taking your dog to the dog park. There are risks to sitting at home, too. I mean, you never know when a plane is going to come through your roof, right? But, seriously, if you take your dog to the dog park your dog is more likely to be injured than if you keep your dog at home.

Your home is a known environment. (If you live in an apartment, not so much, because you have to venture out into the outside world at least three to four times a day and who knows what all those crazy people in the world will think up next…In DC it was bizarre how many times the pup and I found chicken bones in the grass or on the sidewalk. Someone would have their hot chicken wings and just leave the bones there for anyone to find. What the…?)

If you keep your dog at home, once it settles into your house and yard and quits chewing on everything it finds, you're pretty much past the danger zone.

Take your dog to the dog park and you will find a whole new host of potential threats.

Most obvious, of course, is other dogs. Each time you go to the dog park, you will likely encounter dogs you've never met before. Most will be fine, but a handful will not. And sometimes dogs that were fine last time, won't be this time.

(Although that's much more rare it does happen. There's a dog that goes after the pup probably every seventh or eighth time he sees her. Rest of the time, he's just fine.)

So, there's always the potential, no matter how slight, of a dog fight.

Also, depending on the nature of the park, you may be exposing your dog to all sorts of new risks. I don't say this to discourage you from taking your dog to the dog park, I just say it to point out the obvious.

Your basic grassed-in two-hundred-square-foot dog park isn't going to present much hazard to your dog. There might be some plants or sticks your dog can eat that make it sick or it might swallow a tennis ball. (It can happen.) Or someone might break a glass bottle in the parking lot or leave something behind you don't want your dog to eat. But nothing too crazy.

Any dog park that has water in the form of lakes or streams carries with it the risk of water-borne illnesses like giardia. The park I take the pup to has a warning sign up that basically says that they don't guarantee that the water is safe to drink or swim in. In a year and half the pup has yet to get sick from swimming and drinking that water, but I know that there is always that possibility of an issue. The streams that ran through the dog parks in DC had the potential to get contaminated with sewage overflow after big storms and sometimes they'd put up signs warning you to keep your dog away from the water for a few days after it rained.

There's also what's under the surface of the water. People are allowed to fish in the lakes where I take the pup and I've heard of a child that waded into that water and came out with a fishing hook caught on his shorts. Or people throw out cans or bottles or other trash that can harm a dog's paws.

Also, if you're in a cold-weather environment and go to a park with a lake, you need to be aware that the lake may ice over on the surface but not be safe for your dog to walk on. That happens at my park. There are a couple months of the year where the lake is regularly iced over and you could safely walk on it. But within a few days that ice can melt and it's hard to know when it's safe and when it isn't.

(I try to keep the pup off the ice at all times. I know other owners who let their dogs run on the ice or even train their dogs to break the ice. Personally, I'm not willing to risk her getting trapped under the surface. As good a swimmer as she is, I don't think she'd survive that.)

If there's a stream or creek or river running through your dog park, be aware that at certain times of year the water may run too fast for it to be safe for your dog. Glencarlyn flooded when I was taking the pup there and I ended up keeping the pup on leash on one of our visits because I wasn't certain that she'd stay away from the suddenly raging river carrying large branches downstream.

Each time you go to the park, you really should assess the situation and make sure that it's still safe for your dog. This doesn't have to be some long, drawn out process. Just be aware of what the weather is and know what that might mean for your dog park. And look at who's there and what kind of dogs they have with them.

(I was once at a park where a man had brought a dog in heat and the male dog he wanted to have impregnate her. If my dog had been a male dog, we would've left as soon as I found that out.)

Another thing to consider is the wildlife. For the parks I prefer, I always have to consider whether there are animals present that will either harm the pup or may be carrying a disease that can harm her. (That's why getting a rabies shot for your dog is a very, very good idea in the U.S.)

I've seen snakes, frogs, badgers, squirrels, rabbits, bald eagles, and elk at the dog parks I take my pup to. Some seem harmless, but she licked a frog once and it made her all frothy-mouthed. (Supposedly they excrete some sort of nasty chemical to discourage animals from eating them. Fortunately, it didn't seem to leave any lasting harm.) I also know a man whose dog was bit by a rattlesnake. And rabbits and squirrels and other animals, at least near Colorado, have been known to carry things like the plague.

If you're going to go to a park that is "natural" you can't avoid hazards like this. The best you can do is be aware of the issues and warn your dog away from anything that might be a threat. When the pup finds a dead bird on the ground, I immediately yell at her and tell her to get the hell away from it because I don't know what's crawling on that thing. And I keep her away from any snakes even though I think the park I go to only has bull snakes.

I also keep an eye on her and make sure that she isn't acting weird or sick. And if she does show signs that something is wrong with her, then we'll be at the vet the next day. Of course, the list of all the potential issues that could be making her sick is so long it's almost crazy, but I'd trust my vet to figure out what it is and heal her up again.

It's a bit of a trade-off you make, especially if you choose the more wild dog parks. Your dog gets to explore and have a lot more fun than if you both just stayed home, but you are taking risks with your pet's health by taking them to a dog park. My goal is to stay alert and try to protect my pup the best I can while still letting her enjoy herself.

NOT ALL DOG OWNERS ARE NICE PEOPLE

In general, and this really is in general, I think people who like dogs are nicer people than those who don't. (I do have a number of friends who aren't dog people and they're wonderful people, but...you know there's a difference there. I mean, honestly, who turns away from a cute puppy trying to play with them? My friend, Mike, that's who.)

Now, not every person who owns a dog likes dogs. Some people buy dogs for protection or to work a farm. And they treat those dogs as tools that serve a purpose. But those people also aren't going to bring that dog to the dog park with them.

So when you see people at the dog park, you're generally seeing people who love dogs. Love them enough to spend time on the dog's happiness.

(Not always. I've seen a handful of people who take the dog to the park in order to get their own exercise. The dog ends up running frantically behind the person who is completely oblivious to the dog's existence or needs. In those cases, I think the person should just leave the dog at home and go to a normal park, but that's just my opinion. Some people actually run with their dogs, and that's great, but these people are not running with their dogs.)

So, in general, most people you meet at the dog park are going to be friendly and nice people who love dogs. However....

There are a few people who go to the dog park who are just not nice people.

For example. There is an older man who goes to my current dog park. Fortunately, I've only run into him three times, because he is, to me, a very unpleasant person.

The first time I ran into him, my dog stole his dog's ball. I gave it back. He proceeded to make a very offensive joke about Jewish people and stealing things. When I said absolutely nothing, he then explained to me that he was allowed to make jokes like that because someone had nicknamed him something-or-other Jew.

(If you don't understand why that is problematic, understand that it's never a good idea to make offensive comments about entire groups of people or anyone, really.)

The next time I ran into him, he was loud and crude but not as offensive as he'd been the first time. If I hadn't met him before I wouldn't have wanted to spend lots of time with him, but I wouldn't have intensely disliked him.

The third time, I overheard him making some comment to another woman about harassment and something to do with the words her and ass. (No, no, no.)

There are all types in the world and if you're out in public you're likely to run into them. All I can say is I'm glad that most dog parks I've been to don't include people like him. But know that dog parks aren't 100% jerk free.

And sometimes people are rude probably without even meaning to be.

I had some dude make a nasty comment about the pup a few weeks ago. She's close to a hundred pounds, so not tiny by any means. But she's a complete sweetheart, too. She isn't aggressive and if she is playing with a smaller dog she will play down to that dog's level so it doesn't get scared or hurt. And puppies lover her. They always want to play with her.

Well, we walked up on two puppies playing. Always a cute sight. I thought we might pause and watch for a minute. Pup was sniffing at something I probably don't want to know about, so she wasn't even trying to play with them at the time. One of the guys standing there turned to me and said, "It's a dog park, not a bear park."

I'm sure he thought he was very witty.

I thought he was an ass who was basically telling us to go away and leave his puppy alone.

Now, pup and I go to that park almost every day. I'd never seen this guy before. She's also not even close to being the biggest dog that goes to that park. And yet he felt he had to make a rude joke about my dog.

Why?

Who knows. But it happens.

Of course, the great thing about the park we go to is that it's huge, so we were able to move on and never deal with that guy again.

If you go to a smaller park, that's not always an option.

Keep in mind, too, that some people are generally friendly but have problems with certain dogs. I have a big, black dog. Some people think that she's going to attack their dogs the minute they see her. (She's not.)

I've also seen people who were just fine with me and my pup tense up when they saw a different dog approach. Usually Rottweilers or Pit Bulls. If you own one of those breeds, best be prepared for people to act weird around you and your dog, which is really too bad, but it happens.

When I see someone giving the pup the side-eye or trying to lead their dog away from us, I call her back and try to avoid them. No point in confronting someone like that.

And, some people are just going to be territorial assholes. I took the pup to a new dog park for her birthday last year and I swear that every single person at that park was looking at us like, "Why are you here? This is our park." They were perfectly nice to one another, but they gave me and her a wide berth. (And I noticed she was the largest dog there by far even though it was a huge park, so I'm sure we weren't the first pair to be treated that way.)

CASSIE LEIGH

My reaction?
Fine. Whatever. Next park.

FRIENDLY OWNER, FRIENDLY DOG

I will say that I think the attitude of the owner is often reflected in the attitude of the dog. Nice and friendly owners tend to have nice and friendly dogs. Closed-off and rude owners tend to have aggressive dogs.

Not always, but often enough.

I have seen some poor dogs who wanted to say hi to everyone but whose owners just kept walking by without a smile and then yelled for the dog to catch up as soon as they passed. (Usually this happens with younger dogs who haven't been broken of their love of other people or dogs quite yet.)

I don't know that I've ever met a truly aggressive dog that had a warm and friendly owner. I've met a few dogs that liked to jump on people whose owners were incredibly friendly. But snarling, attacking, or mounting other dogs? No.

Not generally.

So my advice would be to pay as much attention to the owner as you do to the dog when you're meeting anyone new. It really is about reading body language a lot of times.

I always try to say hi and smile and also greet the dog.

If I greet the person and they don't smile or say hi back, I know to be more wary of their dog.

If I say hi to the dog and I don't see a tail wag or the dog doesn't come over for a scratch or try to sniff at my dog, I also know to keep my dog away.

It's important to realize, too, that some dogs are dog dogs and some are people dogs. A dog dog will go straight for other dogs and ignore the people. (That's my dog.) A people dog will ignore all dogs to go to a stranger to have its ears scratched. If a dog doesn't do either, it's best left to itself.

I do have a series of signs I watch for to see if a dog is going to be aggressive or react poorly:

SIGNS OF A DANGEROUS OR UPSET DOG

As with the people at dog parks, most of the dogs that are at dog parks are nice and well-socialized. But not all of them are.

So what do I look for when I'm looking for a dog that could be dangerous or who is clearly upset and I should keep the pup away from?

1. Ears back

Not all dogs do this, but many will either put their ears back or their ears will be held very close to the skull or flat. If you look closely, there's a certain amount of tension in the ears which you can recognize in almost any breed.

2. Tail down, straight out, or not moving

Again, depends on the dog, but, generally, a dog that's wagging its tail excitedly back and forth isn't a threat and isn't upset.

Often, a dog that puts its tail down between its legs is nervous not aggressive, but a nervous dog can be a spooked dog and there's no reason to make things worse for it by scaring it further. I always talk softly to dogs like that and am sure, if they let me, to offer my hand to sniff before I even think of petting them.

A dog with its tail tensely held straight out from its body is, to me, generally an aggressive dog that's on alert to maybe attack. If nothing else, it's not at ease, and is best left alone.

You also see sometimes a dog that's sort of wagging its tail, but not really. That is, once again, a nervous dog. I always try to approach with caution and calm.

3. Slouched shoulders

Pup sometimes does this when she's approaching a new dog, so I know it's not really a sign of aggression in every dog. But I think it is a sign of caution and a certain wariness that could mean an attack. If I see a dog with all the other signs and its head is down below shoulder level instead of high, I proceed with caution.

4. Intense stare

If a dog shows some of the other behaviors and its gaze fixes on my pup, I get my pup out of there. That to me is a sign of pending attack. A relaxed dog will look at an approaching dog, look at the lake, look at a bouncing ball, look at its owner etc. If a dog can't take its gaze from another dog, it's either nervous or very aggressive.

5. Snarling

This is an obvious one. If a dog bares its teeth at my dog in a snarl, we're gone. Usually dogs will give a quick flash of their teeth, maybe two seconds or so, when they want to be left alone. They likely won't attack at that stage, but if your dog continues to bother them, it may well be followed by a nip or bite in your dog's direction.

Keep in mind that some dogs do play snarl. There's a difference you'll learn to recognize if you pay attention.

That's just my list of what to look for. I also pay attention to the owner. If the owner is present and paying attention and doesn't show any signs of nervousness or fear, then I assume the dog is friendly, too. (Or the owner is just an idiot, but in that case the owner is probably on their cellphone, talking to someone else, or walking twenty feet ahead of or behind their dog.)

I don't consider barking a sign of threat. Many dogs like to bark just because they're so darned excited that they just can't contain themselves. Or they're a breed that likes to take control of other dogs. Or they're just barkers.

If you listen to enough dogs bark, you will recognize the type of bark that an aggressive dog gives versus a dog that just wants to play.

I also don't consider the belly to the ground thing to be aggressive. (This is when a dog lays down on the ground at the approach of another dog, but is tensed to jump back up.) Pup often does this when she sees another dog she wants to say hi to. She'll stop right where we are, lower herself onto the ground, ready to pounce, and then wait for the dog to approach. She usually jumps back up when the dog is almost on top of her.

I've seen a lot of other dogs do this, too, so I think it's just some sort of weird dog behavior. Kind of a "see, I'm no harm" sort of gesture followed by a "let's play" leap. If your dog does do this, like mine does, I would warn the other dog owner that your dog is going to leap up when they get close so it doesn't startle them.

Sometimes just knowing what's happening can defuse a situation.

DOGS PLAYING WITH OTHER DOGS AT THE DOG PARK

It really depends on the dog park whether people go there expecting their dogs to play or not. I would say that most people take their dog to the dog park expecting that their dog will play with other dogs. But there's an off-leash dog park I take the pup to that's basically a fenced-in hiking trail. I rarely see dogs playing on that trail and owners don't really stop to let their dogs play. They say hi and keep going.

The dog parks that are just squared-off areas of dirt or grass, I think the only reason to go there is so your dog can play.

Again, read the owner as much as the dog to see what they want or expect. Even at my normal dog park where it's pretty standard for people to stop walking to see if the dogs will play with each other there are some people who clearly don't want their dogs to play with other dogs or who aren't going to stop to play.

Here are the rules I try to follow when it comes to my dog playing with other dogs at the park:

If the other dog is on leash, I call my dog away.

If my dog takes someone's toy, I offer to get it back for them.

If the owner seems nervous about my dog playing with theirs (generally an issue with smaller dogs), I call my dog away or offer to do so.

Once my dog and another dog start playing, I stand close enough to the other owner so we can watch and talk about the dogs and I can react if the other owner decides there's a problem.

If my dog is being in any way aggressive with the other dog or the other dog is tail-down, ears back, or crying, I will either (a) immediately step in and pull my dog away or (b) ask the owner if they want me to pull my dog away. (Sometimes dogs play rough together. My rule with the pup is if she keeps going back for more, I'll let her keep playing even if she's getting her ass handed to her or crying like the world is ending, which she does when playing with an Irish wolfhound we know.)

If my dog puts another dog on its back (which happens and is just part of playing most of the time), I will pull my dog off and then release her to keep playing. (I think some dogs who are having fun playing can panic once pinned on their back.)

If my dog mounts another dog, I pull her off. (Only happened once, but pup has had multiple dogs try that on her. She now has a spin move she does that gets them off her, but it's never appreciated. FYI, this is a dominance move, not a sexual thing.)

If my dog is playing chase with another dog and other dogs start to join in so it becomes a situation where one dog is being chased by three or four dogs, I pull my dog away. What was good fun when two dogs were playing can quickly turn into an attack situation.

An important thing to understand is that sometimes dogs play rough. It's not unusual for a dog to pin another on its back. I've seen my dog pinned and seen her pin other dogs. Usually one dog pins the other, they stare at each other, tongues lolling to the side for a second or two, and then they keep playing. But sometimes this becomes an aggressive situation and the dog that's pinned the other dog takes it further by biting or snarling at the pinned dog. In that case, you need to separate the dogs.

I will physically grab my dog by the collar and pull her away if I think it's needed.

It's also not unusual to see dogs showing their teeth at each other while they play. It's different from snarling at each other in that it isn't aggressive. It's more like them running around with their mouth open than baring their teeth in a snarl. You'll learn to recognize the difference, especially in your own dog.

If you do have a dog that tends towards the more aggressive side, be sure you can handle your dog and remove them from the situation if need be. Some people use shock collars or carry spray bottles or whistles or other tools to help them manage their dogs. As I mentioned, I will physically grab my dog and pull her away if I think it's needed. Whatever you do, be prepared to step in and take control of the situation if it warrants it.

THE JUMPING DOG

I mentioned it above, I'm going to mention it again. I don't think it's appropriate to let your dog jump on other people. It generally results in dirty clothing because most dog parks at some point devolve into dirt or mud. And it can hurt people. My mom bruises very easily and a dog jumping on her is bound to leave her with a six-inch bruise that won't go away for a couple of weeks.

So, how do you deal with a jumping dog? Either your own or, as will happen, someone else's?

According to the discipline classes I took, the way to get a dog to stop jumping is to turn away from them or ignore them. That can sometimes work.

I find that I can keep other people's dogs from jumping on me, most of the time, by placing my hands against the dog's chest and holding it down and back.

There's also putting up your knee to block the dog, but I think that one is a little more harmful since it's basically kneeing the dog in the chest. But if the dog won't learn...you have to do something to keep them at bay.

As an owner, if you can't get that behavior under control within a few weeks, don't take your dog to the dog park until you can. It's just rude.

DISCIPLINING OTHER PEOPLE'S DOGS

This is probably a touchy subject. I know people don't like to have their kids disciplined by strangers and I'm sure the same is true with their dogs, but…

If someone's dog is bothering my dog, I will intervene. (I also pet almost every dog I meet at the dog park and greet all of them, so I'm just that person.)

There was a dog for a while there that was obsessed with the pup. Every time it saw her it shadowed her. And it was a giant St. Bernard, too, so it was about one and a half times her size. Scared the pup to death.

Did the owner do anything about it? Nope.

He'd stand about ten feet away and say, "Here Gertie, Gertie. Here Gertie, Gertie." The dog didn't even bother to look at him, let alone listen to him. She'd just keep after my dog. (Who by then was generally hiding between my legs.)

So when that dog got too close, I would gently turn her away from the pup and push her back in the direction of her owner. I didn't hit her or anything like that, but I did push her away or keep her at arm's length so she couldn't reach my pup.

It will happen. Your dog will be threatened or bothered by a dog whose owner won't or can't control it.

I remember witnessing another incident where a Newfie attacked a sweet ten-month-old St. Bernard and pinned it on its back and was snarling in its face. The owner of the Newfie knew she should do something, but she was completely ineffective about it. The St. Bernard's owner and I ended up stepping in to end the situation. (By pulling the dog off and then physically standing between the two dogs.)

I've also had a few dogs try to mount the pup. Actually, more than a few. When she was little and this happened, I stepped in and pulled the dog off her. Now she has a fancy little spin move she does to get them off.

Usually, and you have to be careful if you're going to even try this, you can pull a dog away by the nape of its neck or by the collar at that location. That's the space directly opposite its face. If you hold a dog here, they'll twist their head side to side but not be able to reach your hand. With the pup, if I need to pull her off of something or someone or just drag her away, I grab her collar and her skin at that point.

Be very careful if you do this with a dog you don't know. I know pup's temperament. She's a sweet dog and I've yet to see her in two years actually bite a dog or person. She might show her teeth when playing or turn her head in the direction of something I'm doing she doesn't like (like pulling grass bits out of her toes), but she's not a biter. I can do this with her and know she might fight me, but won't hurt me.

I can't say the same of all other dogs.

And, while I think it's fine to step in to protect your dog, do not do physical harm to another dog unless there's absolutely no other choice. That includes, for example, kicking a dog or hitting it on the head. If your dog is being seriously attacked, then do what it takes to save your dog. But be sure you aren't overreacting to what was really a play situation. (I just heard a story where some guy started whacking a woman's dog on the head because it was sniffing at his dog who'd just come out of the water with a toy in its mouth. Seriously? If you're that paranoid about other dogs interacting with yours, don't go to a dog park.)

POST-PARK CARE

You can't just assume that you can throw your dog in the car, run over to the dog park, let the dog play, come home, and be done.

Often, you're going to need to put in some post-park time to deal with your dog.

First, many dog parks are muddy or dirty. Some dog owners don't want that mud or dirt in their car. (I don't care.) Those people bring a towel with them to the dog park and wipe down their dog's paws before they let the dog into their car.

Me, I just let the pup get in the car. But if her paws are dirty enough, I'll wipe them down with a damp rag once we get home.

Sometimes I decide she's dirty enough that she needs a bath.

Now, if you're lucky, your pup will like those self-serve dog wash places like they have at Petco or other places and you can take your pup there, wash them, and dry them before the dog ever sets foot in your house. My dog hates those places. She will jump out of the four-foot-high bath and run away. That's assuming I can even get her to that part of the store.

But, with a lot of reluctance, she will let me put her in the tub or the shower. So I sometimes have to bring her home, coax her into the bathroom, and then dump water on her feet. She doesn't usually require a full bath, more of a soap and rinse of each paw and maybe the tail.

There's also the issue of water quality. Honestly, I don't worry about it. Pup drinks the water in the rivers and lakes where we go and she swims in that water and I don't worry about rinsing her off. But I've known people who rinse their dogs off before they leave the park or immediately take their dog home and rinse them in the bath or shower so none of that nasty water hangs around.

That also helps when your dog might have run through something like poison ivy.

Honestly, I think the pup is miraculously self-cleaning compared to, say, my hiking boots. They are far more dirty and smelly than she ever is when we get home from the dog park.

The one thing I've found to be the biggest pain is the grass seed or sticky pods that gets caught up in her coat in the summer months. When it's at its worst, I've spent about forty-five minutes removing little pokey bits from her fur and toes throughout the rest of the day. (She doesn't let me do it all at once, so I take three or four different passes at her.)

If you have a dog with a thick coat, like I do, and your dog does run around in high grass or bushes, like mine does, be sure to check your dog over thoroughly. You may not be able to see all the grass bits, but if you run your fingers along the dog's skin you'll feel them.

Be sure to check your dog's underarms and between their toes especially. My pup can usually lick a lot of those bits free with enough effort, but she can't reach under her front legs and she always has a few there. Also, the ones in her toes can get really deep in there to the point I have to use tweezers to remove them.

If you don't remove these things they can irritate your dog's skin or create friction bumps which can be very painful, so definitely check your dog when you get home.

Also, if you're in certain area where ticks or fleas are particularly aggressive, you should check for those, too. I have the pup on flea and tick medicine, which normally works just great. But when we came back from DC we drove through the Deep South and we both ended up with ticks even though she was on the medicine. You don't want to leave those things in there for any length of time. Lyme disease is no joke.

Generally, your dog will let you know there's a problem. For example, pup will lick at a spot where she has a grass seed or tick.

CONCLUSION

That's about it. Taking your dog to the dog park can be a great experience for the dog. And for you. (That's why I like the bigger parks that let me get my exercise at the same time the pup is getting hers.)

Don't let one or two bad experiences put you off. Keep trying until you find a park that works for you and your dog, or a time at that park that works for you.

And do be a responsible dog owner and dog park participant. If we all do our part to be pleasant, control our dogs, and pick up after ourselves, we can all continue to enjoy dog parks for a long time to come.

ABOUT THE AUTHOR

Cassie Leigh is the proud parent of an adorable and incorrigible Newfoundland named Miss Priss who demands to go to the dog park each morning and likes to run around in the long grass and swim in the lake. Miss Priss also has an unerring ability to find dead animals, snakes, and frogs.

www.ingramcontent.com/pod-product-compliance
Lightning Source LLC
Chambersburg PA
CBHW070923130526
44591CB00049B/2110